SOCIAL PET SUPERSTARS OF PETSPAGE

BY KAREN BOSTICK
PetsPage.com

ISBN 978-0-9888417-3-4

PETSPAGE

THIS BOOK IS DEDICATED TO ALL THE AMAZING PEOPLE WHO PARTICIPATE IN KEEPING OUR PETS HAPPY & HEALTHY!

Acknowledgements

I'd like to give a very special acknowledgement to the Ambassadors of PetsPage.com. Tinks & I have been fortunate to have the love and support of so many virtual friends from all around the world who believe in us and work to help grow PetsPage.com's community. They are always active on PetsPage.com and eager to greet and welcome new members. Without their generous support, PetsPage.com would be nowhere near the booming social pet community it is today. Thank you for being Ambassadors of PetsPage.com and extra special Tinks' kisses for you!

PetsPage.com's Ambassadors

Sonja Kennedy and Zack
Sandi Patrick Simmons
Renee Youngblood and Sienna
Amy Handaly and Sammy
Myra Davis and Chloe

Thank you to the talented Derrinita Walker for working with me to create our fun comic book style designed to showcase the Social Pet SuperStars of PetsPage. I'm especially thankful for Laurie Kuntz & Lana Noels for ensuring PetsPage.com's fabulous SuperStars shined brightly in the 1st Edition!
A very special thank you goes out to PetsPage.com's Social Pet Manager, Jane Gonzalez. Jane, you are truly a gift to the world and I'm honored to call you my friend. We love you!
– Karen Bostick & Tinks

PP

PETSPAGE

SOCIAL PET SUPERSTARS OF PETSPAGE

PetsPage.com's Social Pet Community was founded by Karen Bostick with the mission of increasing pet owner awareness for all things happy and healthy for pets today. The Social Pet SuperStars featured in this book are real pets who shined so brightly in PetsPage.com's SuperStar Search that they were voted by fans from all over the world to be featured in our First Edition. We are proud to announce the top Social Pet SuperStars and SuperStars to Watch! A Social Pet is a real pet that has a Social Pet Page on PetsPage.com complete with fans, daily posts and tons of personality!

PetsPage.com

PetsPage.com is a unique social pet community where pet lovers from all around the world come to share, socialize, and most importantly, smile. On PetsPage.com, pet lovers engage directly with each other, as well as pet and veterinary professionals, to share and exchange valuable information in a fun and social way.

See you on PetsPage.com – A Place for Social Pet Lovers!

I love you Mr. Ball!

Social Pet SuperStar
Tinks

Hi everybody! I'm **Tinks** and I love making people smile all over the world! I'm a 10 year old Maltipoo and an IMHA survivor. My very favorite thing ever is playing with Mr. Ball! I live in Boise, Idaho and have two houses. During the week I'm busy making new friends on PetsPage.com and hiking with my mommy, Karen, and on the weekends I'm snuggling and cuddling with my daddy, Scott. **Become a fan of We Love Tinks on PetsPage.com for your daily dose of happiness!**

Nighty night time!! See ya'll in the morning!

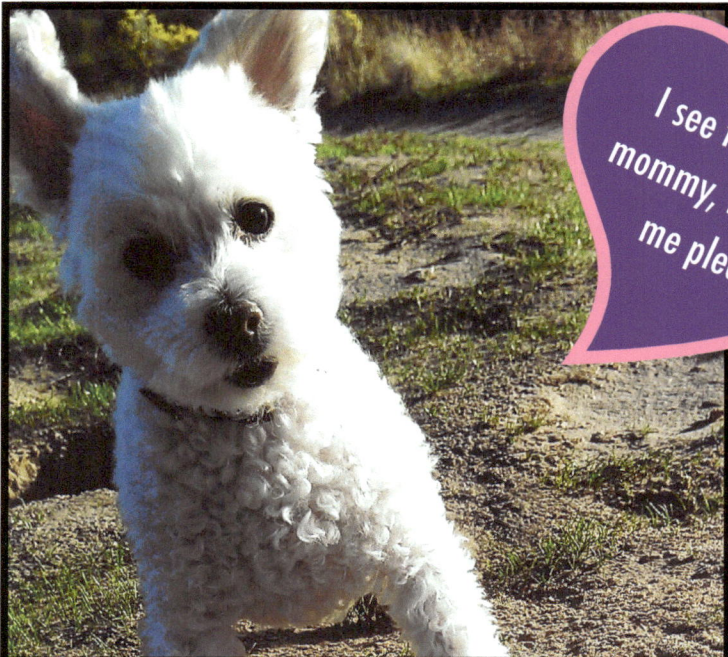

I see that ball mommy, throw it to me please!

Take time to stop and smell the flowers every pawdy.

Good morning! Sending love and snuggles!

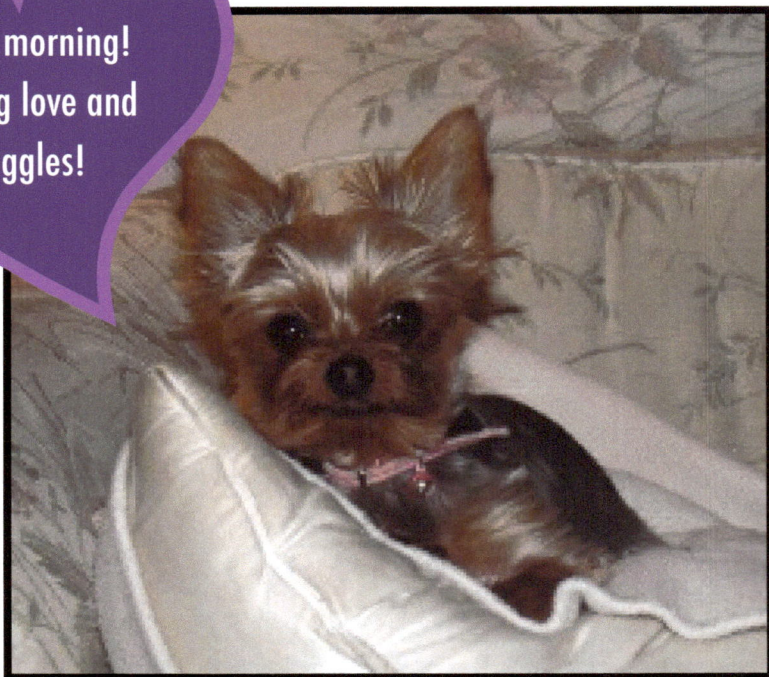

Social Pet SuperStar
Teeny Tiny Tia

Hello everypawdy! My name is Tia and I am a Micro Teacup Yorkie from Alberta, Canada. My barkday is December 13, 2010 and I weigh just under 3 lbs. Puppy kisses are free to all I meet. Cuddling is my favorite thing to do. Mommy has been trying to let the hair on my head hair grow out so it is easier to put in a bow. It does go everywhere since I have such very fine baby-like hair, so I'm excited to get dolled up with my new accessories! Follow Tia at PetsPage.com!

Giving you all a wave hellooooooo!

PP

SOCIAL PET SUPERSTAR
Chloe

Hi, I'm Chloe from Alabama. I like to play with a soft ball and jump up and catch it. I like to bring it to my mom Myra so she can throw it for me, and I bring it back to her! I also like to sit on the window sill and watch birds and squirrels play outside. I love to chase a piece of cat food across the floor and then eat it! Learn more about Chloe at PetsPage.com!

Can we
go to bed now,
Mama?

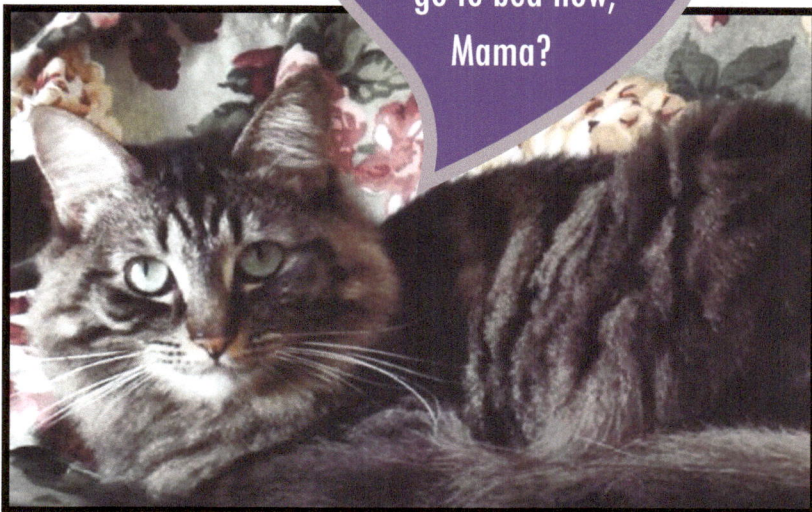

Mama,
why can't I go outside
and play with the birds
and squirrels?

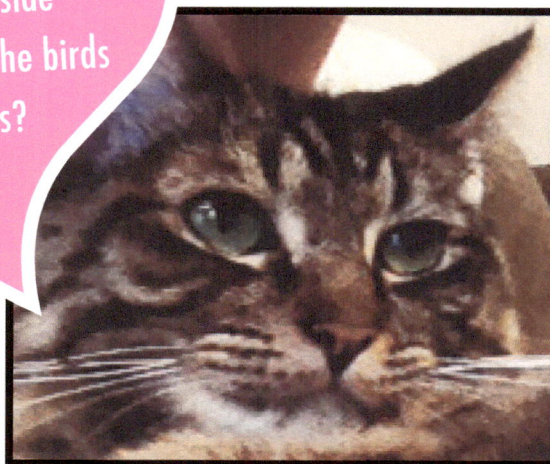

I hope all shelter dogs get a chance to wear a cool bandanna like me someday!

Dogs like me with special needs, and older dogs, make great pets!!

PP

The way I see it, me and my mommy rescued each other.

Social Pet SuperStar
Jojo

My full name is Jojo Crazy Legs Bean. I am a 3.5 pound Chihuahua from Colorado, born with a birth defect. I was surrendered to a shelter which determined that I was unadoptable because my back legs didn't work quite right, and I got marked for euthanasia. But thank goodness a rescue group took me and I was adopted almost 6 months later! I didn't like my wheelchair at first, but once I finally realized that it gave me more freedom, I decided that I like it a lot!! Become a fan of Jojo on PetsPage.com!

Ruby

I'm a Japanese Chin from Arkansas, and I was born on 06/26/2010 with hip dysplasia, a curved spine, and bad knees. My first owner passed away, then I went to a couple of other houses before I found my forever home. I love everyone and have a wheelchair to help me get around sometimes. I love to dress up with my sister Mila. Find out more about Ruby on PetsPage.com!

I love you to the moon and back!

Cowgurl Ruby

Never give up on yourself - every life deserves a second chance.

Just believe dreams do come true!

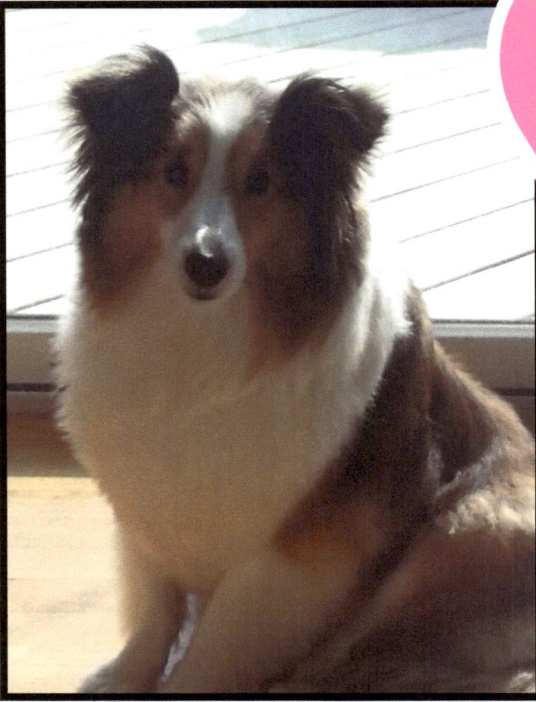

Enough with the picture taking mom!

Do you realize I am a dog, mom? Stop dressing me in these weird clothes!

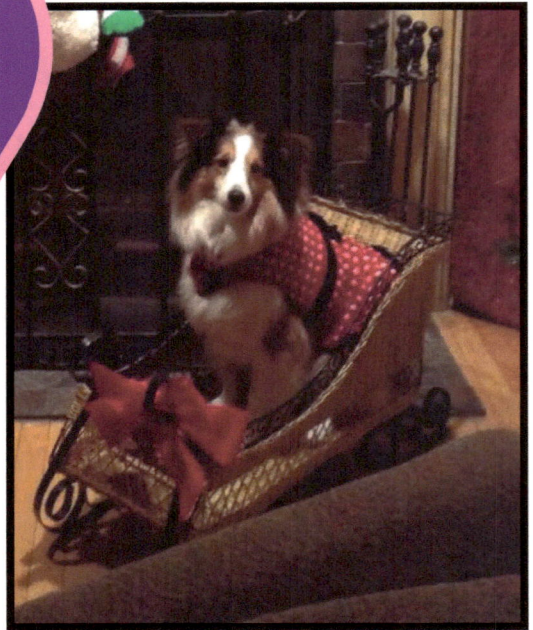

I have a big smile whenever my mom takes me on an adventure!

PP

Social Pet SuperStar
Lola

My name is Lola and I'm from New Jersey. I'm a six year old Shetland Sheepdog who has been with my family since I was six weeks old. I love all treats, but my favorite would have to be True Chews Premium Jerky. Tricks are my specialty and I love striking a pose for the camera. My mom thinks it's funny when I'm laying on my back, and she hits that certain spot, and my leg starts going a mile a minute. Follow Lola at PetsPage.com!

PP

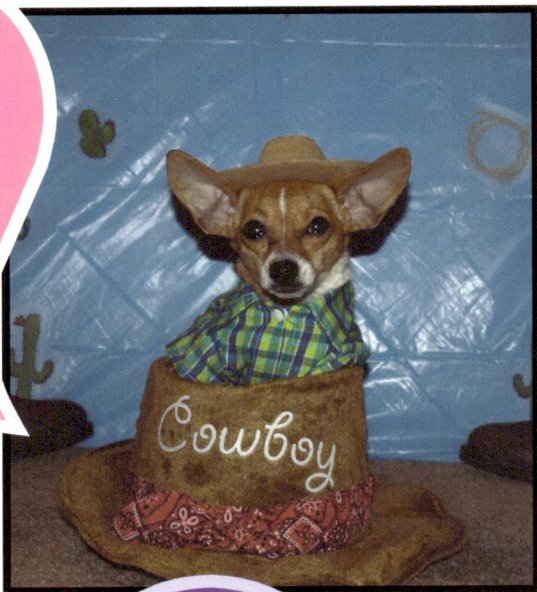

Come on dad! I'm feeling good today, let's play dress up!

Look at me go Dad! Now can I pleeeeaaaase just have a little bite of whatever you're eating?

Social Pet Superstar
Anthony Mater

Hello! I'm Anthony Mater from California. I'm a Chihuahua-Dachshund mix and I have a host of medical issues due to a genetic disease called Legg Perthes, but I enjoy life as best I can. I don't let anything stop me! I cry if I can't see where my Daddy's at, and I love taking pictures. Learn more about Anthony Mater at PetsPage.com!

I love Toy Story and Woody is my best friend.

Being with my furever family is such a delicious feeling!

It's not about who you were, but about who you are now.

Belly rubs make life better.

SOCIAL PET SUPERSTAR
Precious Peanut

I'm a Pomeranian from Arizona and my friends call me Peanut. I spent the first 7 years of my life in a puppy mill as a breeder. I had no idea what life was like outside of a cage until I was rescued and found my furever family earlier this year. My family traveled a long way to meet me and, even though I had not had much human contact, I went right up to my family that morning and claimed them as mine. See, we dogs know these things and I knew that this was where I should have been my whole life. Now about six short months later I am starting to learn how it is to be loved and how to play & love back. Find out more about Peanut on PetsPage.com!

SOCIAL PET SUPERSTAR

Rosie

Hi there! My full name is Roseanne Pandora Daisy Helms, but you can call me Rosie. I'm from Texas. My favorite thing to do is play with my never ending supply of toys. I like to bring them to you and put them down a little bit away from you so you have to reach for it. It's like a game within a game, to see how far away I can put the toy before you stop reaching for it and throwing it. So fun! My best friend is another local Yorkie named Polly Wolly. My mom wasn't originally looking to get a dog, but I was a surprise Christmas present, and from the moment she held me she was hooked for life! Follow Rosie at PetsPage.com!

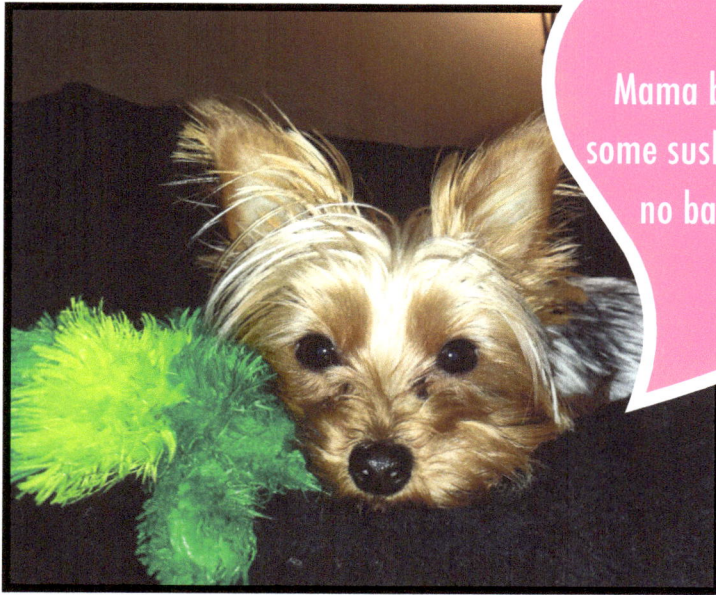

Mama brought home some sushi, but there was no bacon in it. Gross!

I am a great protector of my family from the intruders (squirrels). lol!

23

Brody

Hello! My name is Brody. I'm a Border Collie from Florida. I used to roam the streets and it made me really scared of everything. Luckily I was rescued and then adopted 4 months later. My mom knew I was scared of lots of stuff, so she started teaching me tricks to help me conquer my fears and build my confidence. I now know close to 200 tricks. I even got to be on TV because I'm so good at doing tricks! I've also earned the title of Trick Dog Champion, which I am very proud of. Learn more about Brody at PetsPage.com!

You are beautiful! Will you be my Valentine?

Let's go on a walk so I can sniff everything!

SOCIAL PET SUPERSTAR TO WATCH

Bella

I'm a Toy Poodle from Ohio who LOVES playing fetch, chewing on bones or sticks, and going on walks. I absolutely dislike getting a bath or getting groomed! Sometimes my parents call me Baby Bella or Baby Girl. I have lived with them since I was six weeks old, and I'm three years old now. The day my parents brought me home changed their world. I am very spoiled! I'm a mommy's girl, but I'm happiest when Daddy & Mommy are home together. Find out more about Bella on PetsPage.com

Princess Ellouise

I am Princess Ellouise from Michigan. I'm a spoiled lil' Pit Bull rescue who loves my momma, my two doggie brothers, and my grannie. Grannie always has the yummiest treats! My playful, yet obedient, disposition has changed a lot of people's minds about Pit Bulls, so I'm proud of that. I'm eager to please! I love playing tug of war with my brothers, but my absolute favorite is going for long walks in the country, especially when we walk past the horses. Become a fan of Ellouise on PetsPage.com!

Momma, where is my tiara?

Keep moving forward to your future!

SOCIAL PET SUPERSTAR TO WATCH

Brogan

Hello! My name is Brogan. I am a 4 year old Lhasa Apso from Scotland, and I love to pray, roll over, sit, and beg. I love eating my socks too! I like to help other dogs find homes, so I help my mom support the local animal shelter. I've won some photo contests, as well as a few awards for doing tricks and having a beautiful fur coat, so my mom is really proud of me. I make her smile everyday! Learn more about Brody at PetsPage.com!

Social Pet SuperStar to Watch
Kipton

I came into my mommy's life in 2013 when I was 11 years old. We live in Wisconsin. I spent the majority of my life in a puppy mill, so I have my setbacks from time to time, but my heart is so big and I have such a fighting spirit that each and every day I amaze my mom! I love snuggling with my Yorkie brothers, going for car rides, going on walks, running in the backyard, and eating. I never miss a meal, that's for sure! Most of all I love my mommy! Follow Kipton at PetsPage.com

Hurry up mommy... I am hungry!

PP

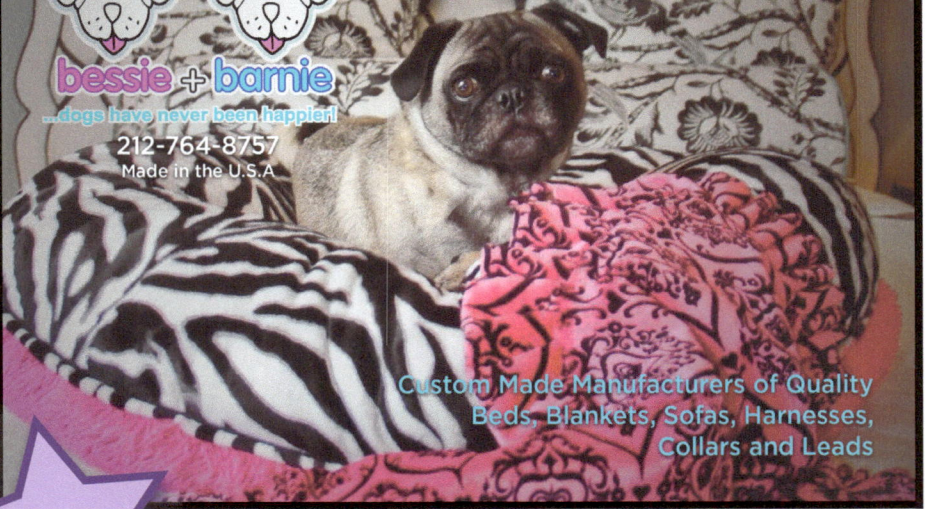

Organic Just Feels Better!

Organic Oscar

Organic Oscar provides pet grooming products to support a holistic and healthy lifestyle for your dogs.

All of our products are:

• FREE of soap, parabens, sulfates, petroleum, dyes, or artificial fragrances.
• Made with certified organic ingredients & essential oils.
• Made in the USA in a solar powered facility.

Made in USA | NO ANIMAL TESTING | Certified Organic

Great for Sensitive Skin

True to our PETS, True to our PLANET, True to our PEOPLE

ECO-MOUSER HEMP

ECO-FETCHER HEMP
ECO-FETCH HEMP
ECO-FETCH HEMP

We provide truly **natural**, toys made of sustainable, durable **hemp** and **wool**. Our hemp products are handmade by disabled adults, and our wool products are handcrafted by impoverished women supporting their families.

Your pets will love them - **guaranteed!**

HONEST PET PRODUCTS®
Pets • Planet • People
www.HonestPetProducts.com

P.O. Box 8988
Green Bay, WI
54308
1-800-790-3385

I'll be a good dog if you buy these for my birthday!

Furtastic deals on stuff I love!